DISCOVERIES IN PALAEONTOLOGY

PACHYRHINOSAURUS

The Mystery of the Horned Dinosaur

MONIQUE KEIRAN

ROYAL TYRRELL MUSEUM

VICTORIA • CALGARY • VANCOUVER

Heritage House Publishing Company Ltd.
#108 – 17665 66A Avenue
Surrey, BC V3S 2A7
www.heritagehouse.ca

Library and Archives Canada Cataloguing in Publication

Keiran, Monique
    Pachyrhinosaurus : the mystery of the horned dinosaur / Monique Keiran.

ISBN 1-894974-03-4

1. Dinosaurs—Juvenile literature. I. Title.
QE862.O65K43 2006   j567.915   C2005-907750-6

Edited by SKB
Proofread by Corina Skavberg
Book and cover design by John Luckhurst
Front cover photo by Darren LeBeuf
All interior photos provided by Royal Tyrrell Museum of Palaeontology, Al Lakusta, Monica Nash, and Collin Orthner.
All interior illustrations provided by Donald Mah and Melanie Wilson.

Printed and bound in Hong Kong

Heritage House acknowledges the financial support for its publishing program from the Government of Canada through the Book Publishing Industry Development Program (BPIDP), Canada Council for the Arts, and the British Columbia Arts Council.

Canada Council   Conseil des Arts
for the Arts   du Canada

BRITISH
COLUMBIA
ARTS COUNCIL
We acknowledge the support of the Province of British Columbia through the British Columbia Arts Council

Alberta

ROYAL TYRRELL
MUSEUM

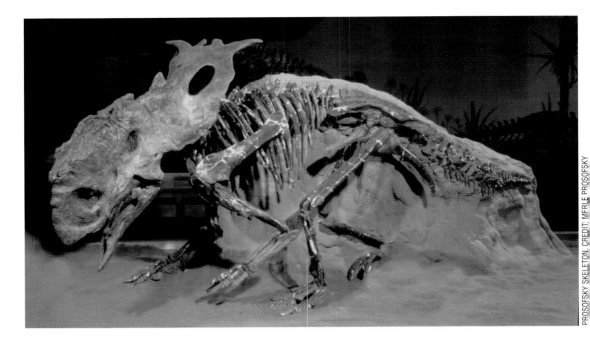

PROSOFSKY SKELETON. CREDIT: MERLE PROSOFSKY

Acknowledgements

The plants, dinosaurs, and other animals illustrated in this book reflect the fossil record of Alberta. Stories and illustrations have been reviewed and approved by scientists at the Royal Tyrrell Museum of Palaeontology.

Scientific advisers: Dr. Dennis Braman (Palaeobotany/Palynology), Dr. Don Brinkman (Vertebrate Palaeontology), Dr. Philip Currie (Dinosaur Palaeontology), Dr. David Eberth (Sedimentary Geology), and Dr. Bruce Naylor (Vertebrate Palaeontology).

Photos: Royal Tyrrell Museum of Palaeontology, Al Lakusta, Monica Nash, and Collin Orthner.

Illustrations: Donald Mah and Melanie Wilson.

Thanks are also due to: Lindsay Cook, Clive Coy, Tammy Kirby, Eva Koppelhus, Becky Kowalchuk, Ken Kucher, Marilyn LaFramboise, Al Lakusta, Vien Lam, Scott Mair, Jim McCabe, Michael Ryan, Elaine Secord, Sue Sommerville, Darren Tanke, and Kathryn Valentine.

The *Pachyrhinosaurus* bonebed was discovered by Al Lakusta. Tyrrell technicians Jim McCabe, Darren Tanke, and Ken Kucher excavated it from 1986 to 1989, assisted by volunteers Bert Hunt, Hans Larsson, Desh Mitra, and Michele Rosteck, among others. The gallery display was designed, made, and assembled by Donna Sloan, Darren Tanke, Ken Kucher, and Fred Orosz.

Contents

Discovery

Horned Dinosaur
Jackpot, 1986

The hard layer of rock followed the cliff top, then stopped.

Jim McCabe was dismayed. If the rock ended, the layer of **fossils** beneath it probably ended as well, and much of the work he and Darren Tanke had done would be for nothing.

It was June 1986. McCabe and Tanke were science technicians from the Royal Tyrrell Museum of Palaeontology, in Drumheller, Alberta. Their mission here, high on a bank above Pipestone Creek, a 12-hour drive northwest of Drumheller, was to dig through dirt, mud, and rock to a layer of dinosaur bones. What they found would determine whether the museum explored the site further.

McCabe and Tanke knew where to find the fossils. A 12-centimetre-thick layer of bones striped the bank, 10 metres above the creek. The fossils were part of a **bonebed**, a jumbled collection of many animals' remains.

McCabe and Tanke knew what dinosaur the bones belonged to. It was *Pachyrhinosaurus* [PACK-ee-RY-noh-SOR-us]—one of the rarest, least understood **horned dinosaurs**. The site at Pipestone Creek promised to yield remains of dozens—even hundreds—of

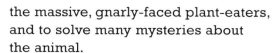

Opposite page: Wapiti River.

Left: Forest cloaks much of northwestern Alberta's fossil riches, making them difficult to find. Where creeks and rivers cut through the region's foothills, remains of ancient plants and animals erode from the banks.

Left: Pipestone Creek flows into the Wapiti River, one of the waterways that drains northwestern Alberta's foothills.

Right: Jim McCabe removing overburden.

the massive, gnarly-faced plant-eaters, and to solve many mysteries about the animal.

But the abrupt end to the layer of hard siltstone that had capped and protected the bones threatened the success of the expedition. McCabe and Tanke had spent three days digging a test pit two metres wide, six metres long, and three metres deep down to the bone layer. The protective siltstone covered only two-thirds of the pit bottom. If that rock had **eroded** long ago, many of the fossils that had once lain in the bonebed may also have washed away.

Hoping he was mistaken, McCabe explored the pit floor further. After about an hour, his trowel hit something hard in the dirt. He uncovered a section of fossil bone. What a relief! The bone layer continued where the siltstone did not.

McCabe uncovered more of the bone. It was flat and wide, with a texture he

recognized from fossils he had found on other dinosaur digs.

"Look at this, Darren. I've found a piece of **frill**."

The long, bony headdresses that swept back over horned dinosaur necks are called frills. Resembling war bonnets, they are decorated with scallops, spikes, bumps, and twisting horns. Each **species** had its own unique set of frill decorations: **Palaeontologists** use them to identify different kinds of horned dinosaurs. In 1986, when McCabe and Tanke explored the Pipestone Creek bonebed, *Pachyrhinosaurus*'s frill was unknown. Scientists knew of only small fragments—not enough to show what the headdress looked like.

The bone McCabe found was one of the most sought-after parts of a *Pachyrhinosaurus* skeleton.

Its discovery was an exciting new beginning for a site first found more than a decade earlier by a local schoolteacher.

Within days of clearing tonnes of bush, dirt, and rock from above the bonebed layer, technician Jim McCabe discovered what would turn out to be the first-known, near-complete fossil of a Pachyrhinosaurus *frill.*

Pachyrhinosaurus and the Horned Wonders

Horned dinosaurs are named for the long, dangerous-looking horns on their faces. *Centrosaurus* (SEN-troh-SOR-us, or Sharp-Pointed Reptile), for instance, carried a half-metre-long horn on its nose, and *Triceratops* (try-SAIR-uh-TOPS, or Three-Horned Face) had horns up to a metre long growing out of its eyebrows.

Horns, however, do not make a horned dinosaur. What separates these dinosaurs from all others is a bony, parrot-like beak. When the dinosaurs were alive, the beaks were covered in **keratin**, the same tough, flexible protein that makes up fingernails and bird beaks.

Pachyrhinosaurus was a horned dinosaur. It had the beak. It also had a triangular head, as other horned dinosaurs had. It had a bony headdress, or frill, growing out of the back of its skull, as most other horned dinosaurs had. It was huge. An adult *Pachyrhinosaurus* measured about six metres from nose to tail, and weighed as much as a schoolbus. It ate plants. It lived during the last half of the **Cretaceous** Period, the last period of time in the 150-million-year Age of Dinosaurs. In many ways, *Pachyrhinosaurus* was like any other horned dinosaur that once lived in North America.

But *Pachyrhinosaurus* was different in one striking way. Instead of the sweeping lances found on fossil *Triceratops* and *Centrosaurus* faces, gnarly platforms of bone cover *Pachyrhinosaurus*'s nose and eyebrows. These bony fossil shields give the dinosaur its name: *Pachyrhinosaurus* means Thick-Nose Reptile.

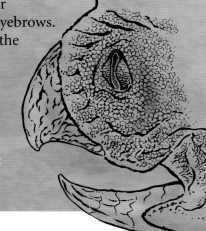

Being a horned dinosaur is all in the beak—a parrot-like beak once covered with keratin.

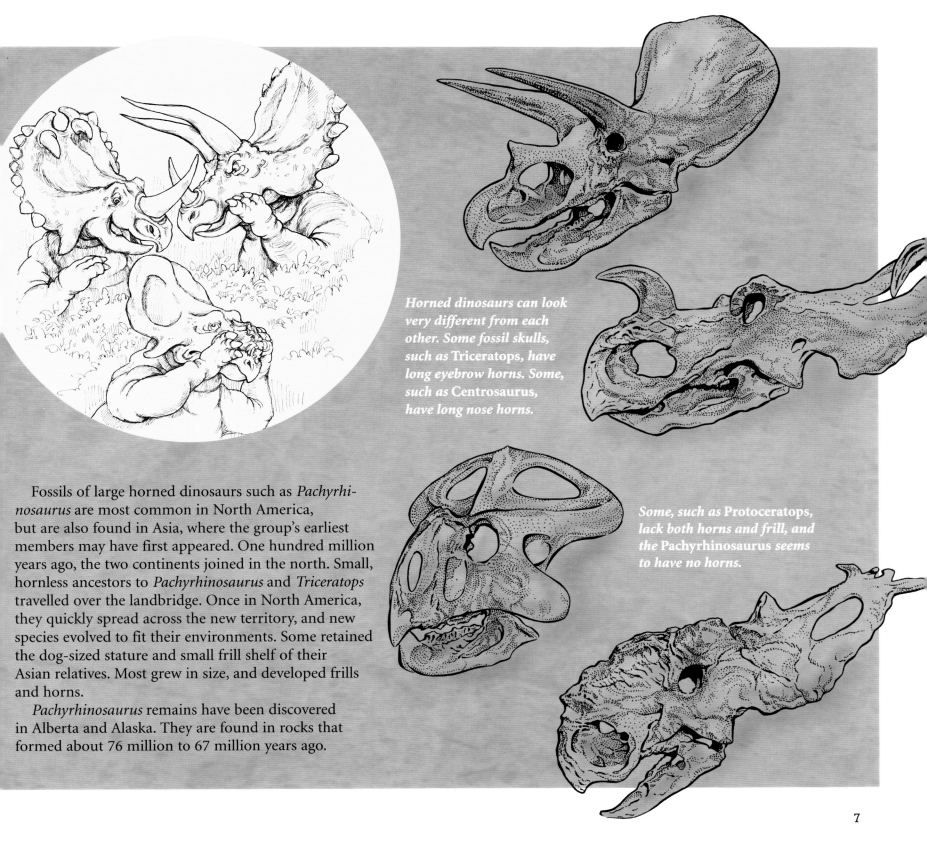

Fossils of large horned dinosaurs such as *Pachyrhinosaurus* are most common in North America, but are also found in Asia, where the group's earliest members may have first appeared. One hundred million years ago, the two continents joined in the north. Small, hornless ancestors to *Pachyrhinosaurus* and *Triceratops* travelled over the landbridge. Once in North America, they quickly spread across the new territory, and new species evolved to fit their environments. Some retained the dog-sized stature and small frill shelf of their Asian relatives. Most grew in size, and developed frills and horns.

Pachyrhinosaurus remains have been discovered in Alberta and Alaska. They are found in rocks that formed about 76 million to 67 million years ago.

Horned dinosaurs can look very different from each other. Some fossil skulls, such as Triceratops, *have long eyebrow horns. Some, such as* Centrosaurus, *have long nose horns.*

Some, such as Protoceratops, *lack both horns and frill, and the* Pachyrhinosaurus *seems to have no horns.*

7

Horned Dinosaur Tales:
The Herd

The dinosaur family had been travelling for weeks. It followed instinct, food, and the young *Pachyrhinosaurus*'s grandmother—a huge, ill-tempered dinosaur who ruled over her daughters, their daughters, and their children, and always knew where to find water and food. The family met the larger herd while still moving through the hills, and began its descent into the great river basin where the young dinosaur and her nest mates had hatched two summers before. As they went, they joined other families and herds trickling out of the hills.

The young dinosaur shoved her mother's side. She fought to keep her place among the moving legs and bodies. Around her, more dinosaurs moved—older siblings, younger siblings, cousins, aunts, second cousins ... In every direction, as far as the young dinosaur could see, dinosaur legs swung and plodded.

Terrified bellows came from one side. The young *Pachyrhinosaurus* couldn't see what was happening, but she felt the herd react. Fear and panic rippled through the herd. Dinosaurs pressed in around her and her siblings. They moved so close the young dinosaur had to fight to keep out from under their feet. The dinosaurs began to run.

Ten thousand thundering footsteps shook the ground as the dinosaurs swept through the shallow valley. The young dinosaur could barely keep up.

She tried to follow the sound of her mother's calls, but the crush of dinosaurs was so great, she struggled just to stay on her feet. Squealing with terror, one of her younger brothers stumbled and fell.

As one, the dinosaurs swung around in a great arc. Separated from her family, the young dinosaur found herself near the herd's edge. She ran just inside the protective ring of adults. Through their legs, she saw the herd's trail swing into view. Their track was a wide, muddy highway pounded through green ferns and weeds. Picking their way through the muck, an **Albertosaurus** pack scoured the path. These giant carnivores were cunning **predators**. They had caused the herd to stampede, hoping an old, weak, or sick horned dinosaur would be left behind, alone and defenceless against their ferocious hunger.

The herd completed its sweeping turn. Speeding up, the dinosaurs lowered their heads. They showed their frills and horns. They charged.

The enraged river of horned dinosaurs bore down on the hunters. For one startled moment, the predators froze. Then the lead *Albertosaurus* roared, and they dashed for safety.

The horned dinosaurs chased them, then slowly, slowly came to a stop. The herd was safe again ... for the time being.

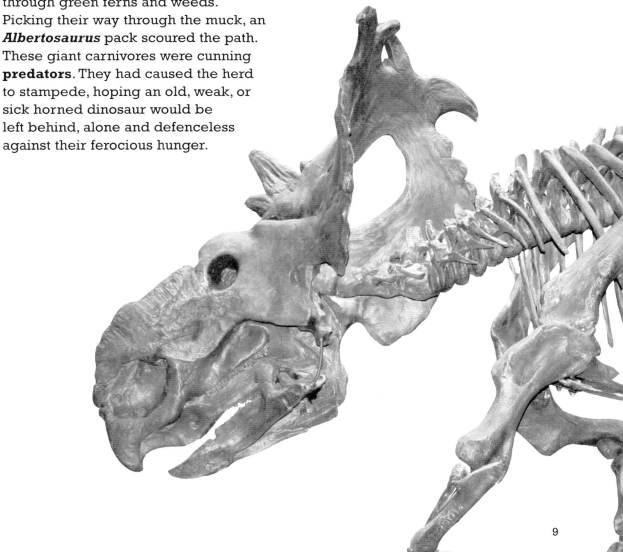

Dinosaurs Up the Creek

Pipestone Creek rushes through the foothills south of the city of Grande Prairie, in northwestern Alberta. A seasonal stream, the creek depends on snow and rain that falls along its twisting canyons and tributaries. Fast-flowing water fills the streambed every spring and cuts into its banks and cliffs, freeing fossils that had lain buried for millions of years.

By August, the creek is nearly dry.

Grande Prairie schoolteacher and fossil hunter Al Lakusta frequently followed streams to find the region's best fossil sites. In September 1973, he took friends to see ancient plant remains preserved in a cliff near the mouth of Pipestone Creek. Curious about what lay beyond, they climbed up the creek.

Several hundred metres past the plant-fossil site, they found fragments of dinosaur ribs lying in the streambed.

Lakusta and his friends scanned the surrounding cliffs. On the northeast side, bits of bone littered the shale-and-sandstone layers of the bank. Above them, 10 metres up, dinosaur bones poked out of the cliff.

A trail of fossil fragments in the creek bed and along the bottom of the bank led Lakusta and his friends to find the layer of dinosaur bones.

Mystery Dinosaur

Alberta's first full-time dinosaur palaeontologist, Philip Currie, travelled to Grande Prairie in 1979 to look at fossils Lakusta had collected from Pipestone Creek.

Currie was intrigued by one of the skull fragments in the collection Lakusta had donated to the local museum. The bone was small and broken. He could not be certain, but he thought it might include part of the bony core of a horned dinosaur's horn.

Currie returned to Grande Prairie in 1983. He and technicians Gary Stonely and Darren Tanke hiked up Pipestone Creek to the fossil site. Bones jutted out from the cliff from a layer that stretched 60 metres along the bank—more than half the length of a football field. Dark brown fossil fragments lay scattered at the bottom of the cliff. The fossil layer was a bonebed. It contained mixed-up remains of many dinosaurs.

The crew searched among the fossils along the cliff for skull bones. A dinosaur's skull contains more information about the animal than any other

The dinosaur fossils eroded out of the cliff about 10 metres above the creek bed and three metres below the cliff top.

part of its skeleton. If they found the right piece of skull, they could identify what kind of dinosaur was buried in the cliff. Currie and the technicians found frill fragments and two skull pieces that had once encased dinosaur brains. The bones confirmed the animals were horned dinosaurs. They even told

Currie the Pipestone Creek animals were closely related to *Centrosaurus,* a dinosaur with a half-metre-long horn on its nose, whose fossils are frequently found in southern Alberta.

But the fossil fragments told no more secrets. The crew could not identify the dinosaur's species.

Pipestone Creek— Now and Then

Pipestone Creek is one of countless streams that drain the foothills of north-western Alberta. The creek cuts through dense forests of spruce, pine, and poplar before it empties into the Wapiti River, 25 kilometres south of the city of Grande Prairie.

The region is very different today from the landscape *Pachyrhinosaurus* roamed

76 million years ago. Then, a shallow sea stretched across North America from the Arctic to the Gulf of Mexico. Parts of Alberta not underwater formed a broad, low-lying plain that separated coast from hill country to the west. The region that is now Pipestone Creek and Grande Prairie lay on the plain. A wide, slow-moving river, hundreds of metres across, snaked across the land. During storms, the river often spilled over its low banks and spread across the countryside, charting new channels through sand-banks, ponds, and marshes, and rearranging the land.

The region around Grande Prairie, Alberta, that contains countless remains of ancient plants, dinosaurs, and other animals little resembles the landscape in which those creatures lived. Where forest now covers hills and creeks cut through narrow canyons, a broad, flat river plain sloped gently toward the sea, a few hundred kilometres away.

D. Mah
04

Fossil evidence suggests that 76 million years ago, the Pipestone Creek area had cooler winters than did regions farther south in Alberta. Fewer fossils of cold-sensitive animals, such as turtles and crocodiles, are found there than in Dinosaur Provincial Park, 1,200 kilometres to the southeast.

Beginning about where the Alberta–British Columbia border stands today, low hills climbed gently into the west. These were the ancestors of today's Rocky Mountains. The hills' distance from the coast meant the highlands were drier than the plains and were home to fewer plants. Temperatures were more extreme—hotter in the dry season, and cooler in winter. During the dry season, the hill country may have become parched and desert-like from lack of rain.

The climate was mild. Although North America was closer to the North Pole than it is today, temperatures in Alberta rarely fell below freezing. Northern Alberta, including Pipestone Creek, included territories of some of the

Taking Dinosaurs Home

Al Lakusta collected dinosaur fossils from Pipestone Creek from 1974 until 1979. At that time, anybody could dig up dinosaur bones in Alberta and take them home.

The rules changed in 1978, when the Alberta government adopted some of the toughest fossil laws in the world. To dig up any fossil in the province today, you must first get permission from the government. The regulations help protect the province's fossils and the scientific information they contain. It also ensures palaeontologists have access to ancient remains.

When the law came into effect, Lakusta donated his fossil collection to the Grande Prairie Pioneer Museum, and to the local college and high school, where the bones could be studied and used in teaching. The museum transferred its share of Lakusta's dinosaur bones to the Royal Tyrrell Museum in 1985.

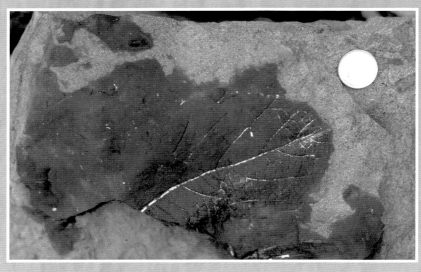

Pipestone Creek has long been known to be the site of many plant fossils, including preserved leaves of gingkoes and ancient flowering plants.

animals and plants that lived farther south in warmer, lusher regions, as well as of creatures that made their homes in cooler northern climates. Unlike southern Alberta, however, in the north scientists find fewer fossils of turtles, crocodiles, and other animals that cannot survive prolonged cold. Nonetheless, differences in sunlight during the year probably played a greater role than temperature in determining seasons. Many plants adapted to the extremes by dropping their leaves at the start of each dark, rainy winter and regrowing them in the spring as the amount of sunlight increased, just as many northern plants do today.

Although little is known about specific plants that grew in the Pipestone Creek region when *Pachyrhinosaurus* lived there, plants were plentiful: The rock along the creek preserves countless tiny fossils of plant pollens and spores, and the plant-fossil site that drew Lakusta and his friends to Pipestone Creek in 1973 contains fossil leaves. At the bonebed, technicians discovered a tree trunk and

roots that had turned to coal, as well as amber and strange, lentil-shaped fossil seeds. Scientists believe primitive sequoia, redwood, cypress, and gingko grew in the region, as well as early broadleaved trees such as maple and sycamore. Ferns, club mosses, some hardy shrubs, and flowering

plants such as lilies and gingers likely colonized the sandbanks and mudflats of the ancient river basin.

Then, as now, ancient Pipestone Creek's wetlands would have been home to many different animals. Birds and winged reptiles ruled the sky. Crocodiles, **champsosaurs** [CHAMP-soh-sors], and turtles lived along the riverbank, although in lesser numbers than in the south. Small mammals that resembled today's shrews scurried around at dusk and at night. The dominant animals of Cretaceous Alberta's landscapes were dinosaurs. Armoured dinosaurs, duckbilled dinosaurs, and horned dinosaurs fed on plants. Large meat-eaters *Daspletosaurus* [dah-SPLEE-toh-SOR-us] and *Albertosauria* [al-BERT-oh-SOR-us], small *Troodon* [TRUE-oh-don], and sickle-clawed **dromaeosaurs** [DROH-mee-oh-sors] hunted across the flood plains for animals to eat.

Pachyrhinosaurus!

Darren Tanke, a technician on Currie's scouting trip, returned to Grande Prairie in 1985. He had heard the city's museum wanted to get rid of its collection of dinosaur fossils, and he wanted to make sure the Pipestone Creek bones would not be lost.

Museum staff showed him the fossils. Everything was still there from two years earlier, when he, Philip Currie, and Gary Stonely had examined them. There were leg bones, foot bones, ribs, skull pieces, bones from both the spine and the tail....

But there was something else—something the crew hadn't seen in 1983. It was a large, oval chunk of bone with two thick prongs. It was the same colour as Lakusta's fossils. The bits of rock clinging to it matched the rock on the Pipestone Creek fossils. It, too, came from the bonebed.

Tanke picked it up. The museum volunteer who was with him said,

"Nice **vertebra**, huh?"

Tanke turned it over, and froze. Moments passed before he could speak.

"This isn't a vertebra," he managed to say. "It's part of a skull."

He looked up at the volunteer. "It's the nasal boss of a *Pachyrhinosaurus*."

Pachyrhinosaurus was one of the rarest, most mysterious horned dinosaurs known. Only four skulls were known. All were from southern Alberta. All were incomplete. One thing they had in common were distinctive, bony platforms on the nose and eyebrows where other horned dinosaur skull fossils had horns.

Tanke held one of the nose platforms in his hands.

If it were from the Pipestone Creek bonebed, the remains of dozens—possibly hundreds—possibly *thousands*—of one of North America's least-known horned dinosaurs lay buried 25 kilometres from where Tanke stood.

Barely able to contain his excitement, Tanke telephoned Philip Currie. When the Royal Tyrrell Museum of Palaeontology opened its doors to the public for the first time later that year, plans were made to send an expedition to Grande Prairie the following summer. What the field crew found at the bonebed would determine whether Pipestone Creek received further attention.

Pachyrhinosaurus is unique among horned dinosaurs for the thick platforms of bone covering its nose and eyebrows. Darren Tanke identified the dinosaur remains buried in the Pipestone Creek bonebed from a nose platform stored at the Grande Prairie museum.

The two skulls discovered in the first weeks of digging at Pipestone Creek were nearly complete. They included not only the different bones that together make a skull but parts of the dinosaurs' frills as well, providing answers to questions scientists had long been asking about Pachyrhinosaurus.

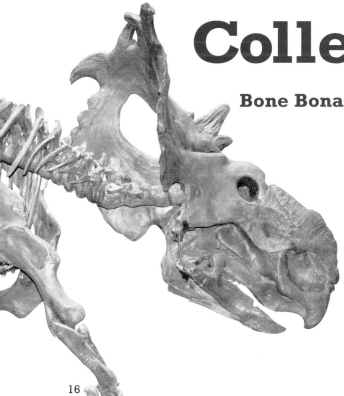

Collection

Bone Bonanza, 1986

McCabe's discovery of the frill fossil in the unprotected part of the test **quarry** was soon followed by another. One week later, Tanke found a large skull bone that had once surrounded a dinosaur's eye. As the technicians dug around the fossils, they uncovered countless other bones. Mixed in with the broken dinosaur ribs, leg bones, and back bones were skull fragments. The technicians found jaw bones, cheekbones, **braincases,** and bits of frill and forehead. The crew even found skull bones from teenaged and baby pachyrhinosaurs.

It soon became clear that McCabe's frill fossil and Tanke's eye-socket bone were different from the other skull fossils. Both were attached to nearly complete skulls. Tanke's skull missed cheekbones and most of the frill. However, the frill's skull-shelf was attached. Right in the middle of the dinosaur's forehead, a bone spike 12 centimetres long curved up: *Pachyrhinosaurus* had horns, after all.

McCabe's frill was attached to a *Pachyrhinosaurus* skull more complete than the one Tanke was uncovering.

These were important finds. Because of them, the Royal Tyrrell Museum of Palaeontology decided the bonebed needed further exploration. McCabe hired someone to clear **overburden** from the entire fossil layer at the end of the field season. Using backhoes and other heavy equipment, the contractor was told to remove hundreds of tonnes of dirt, rock, and brush that buried the bonebed on that side of the creek. The resulting dig site would be eight times the size of McCabe and Tanke's test pit.

Dinosaur Graveyards

Palaeontologists study fossils to understand ancient plants and animals, and the environments they lived in. While every fossil adds to our knowledge of past worlds, few fossil sites offer clearer pictures of what and how different ancient animals lived together than bonebeds do.

A bonebed contains bones from many individual animals that accumulate in one place. It may represent the slow buildup of bones over several years—for instance, on a river's sandbar that snags bones or dead animals out of the current. These bonebeds contain remains of many different kinds of animals that lived in a region. The fossil sites provide palaeontologists with information about entire animal communities—all the animals that lived in an area.

Bonebeds that contain bones of only one kind of animal are snapshots of species' **biology** and behaviour. Each site may represent a group of animals that died together in a sudden, deadly event, such as a flood, dust storm, or volcanic eruption. Buffalo-kill sites, where Native North Americans drove herds of buffalo over cliffs to their deaths, are examples of this kind of bonebed.

These dinosaur bonebeds represent entire social or family groups that

Rivers and streams may carry any kind of bone or animal on their currents. Sandbars that slow the water also capture whatever is floating in the water. Fossil bonebeds that form this way preserve information about animal communities that once lived in an area.

One of the best-known dinosaur bonebeds is the Centrosaurus bonebed in Alberta's Dinosaur Provincial Park. Discovered in 1977, it contains remains of more than 300 centrosaurs that palaeontologists believe died in a flood 75 million years ago.

A prehistoric predator trap lies in the heart of central Utah, in the United States. Of the 60 or so dinosaurs whose remains have been found at Cleveland-Lloyd Dinosaur Quarry, almost 45 were large meat-eating dinosaurs.

probably lived together for part of their lives or part of each year. For example, the Pipestone Creek *Pachyrhinosaurus* site contains remains of baby dinosaurs, as well as bones of teenaged and adult pachyrhinosaurs. The range in growth sizes tells scientists how quickly dinosaurs in that particular species grew and how they changed as they grew.

Predator traps are the rarest bonebeds. They contain bones of many carnivorous animals and few remains of plant-eating animals. The bones collect in places from which animals cannot escape, such as quicksand or sinkholes. An animal— plant-eater or meat-eater—gets stuck and dies. The smell of its rotting body attracts meat-eaters, who come to feed, become trapped, and die. Their rotting, stinking bodies attract more meat-eaters …

Predator-trap bonebeds provide information about biology and behaviour of ancient meat-eating animals.

Horned Dinosaur Tales:
Summer Days

The young *Pachyrhinosaurus* rolled over in the water. She rubbed her back in the mud and leaves lying on the bottom of the river. The mud soothed itchy insect bites. She twisted upright, and cool water slid over her hide. Shaking water from her face, she bit off a mouthful of weed floating near the bank and looked around at the other young, bathing horned dinosaurs.

Far better to be here with her nestmates and cousins where it was cool and there were tender, tasty greens to eat than to be with the adults. Since before the start of the spring migration, the bulls had fought constantly. They shoved. They wrestled. They peed all over the place. They dug up and rolled in the best feeding areas. Even from here, out of sight and some distance away, she could hear their bellows and their grunts, even though the mating season was over.

And now that the herd had reached its summer territories and had split into family groups, the cows were as mean as the bulls. Every time the young *Pachyrhinosaurus* approached, her mother nipped her—hard!—on the frill or hip. Any time she wandered too close to one of her aunts or older sisters, they shoved her away. They were building nests and getting ready to lay the year's eggs. They had no time for almost-grown children who could look after themselves.

The young *Pachyrhinosaurus* was too old to be mothered and too young to be a mother. She and her nestmates had no status or power within the herd. Her thin, delicate baby horns had split and flattened since the dinosaurs had arrived at their summer territories. Her frill had grown longer and wider, its pie-crust edges replaced by curls and horns. It would be another year before she acquired the face of a grown *Pachyrhinosaurus*—gnarled masses of bone padding her nose and eyebrows, bumps of bone on her lip, and horns on her face and forehead. It would be another year before she could mate and lay eggs. At three summers old, the young *Pachyrhinosaurus* was a teenager.

Not fitting in with the family, she hung around with other teenagers from the herd. They shadowed and circled the family, never too close to be bullied by breeding relatives, yet never far from the herd's protection.

It was peaceful here at the watering hole on the river's edge, away from the herd. The dinosaur tore off another mouthful of water weed and climbed up the bank into the heat.

Recipe for a Fossil

Only living things can become fossils. First, however, they must die. Organisms that are still alive—no matter how old or crotchety—are not fossils. After organisms die, their remains must be buried deep within layers of **sediment** such as sand, silt, or mud. They must remain buried.

Prolonged burial slows rot and allows chemical changes and mineral deposits that happen when a **specimen** becomes a fossil. The fossilization process called **replacement** occurs when **organic** molecules within the remains change into non-organic minerals. **Permineralization** is a second fossilization process. During permineralization, minerals in water seeping through the ground fill tiny cracks and holes within the remains, gradually turning once-living tissues to stone. Specimens preserved in ice or amber can also become fossils if they last long enough.

Fossils are remains and traces of life at least 10,000 years old. Anything

Given enough time and the right conditions, any living thing or its traces may fossilize. Of the countless living things that have lived on the planet, only an infinitesimal number has been preserved, and remained preserved for more than 10,000 years.

that lives or once lived—plant, animal, fungus, bacterium—may become a fossil. However, of all the things that ever lived, only a very, very, *very* small number do fossilize.

Jigsaw Quarry

Every time McCabe and Tanke tried to uncover more of the massive skulls, other fossils got in the way. Shoulder bones poked through eye sockets. Toe bones were wedged within jaw bones. Ribs wrapped around the surfaces of leg bones. Each fossil had to be mapped, untangled, removed, and **catalogued** before excavation could continue. As many as 150 bones packed every square metre of the bonebed. There were more fossils than rock. The bones were so tangled the technicians could not remove one bone without excavating a dozen others overlapping and wrapping around it. And each of those dozen bones twined around another dozen bones.

Many of the fossils were in pieces; others broke as soon as the technicians lifted them. During the 76 million years since the bones had first collected in the bonebed, millions of tonnes of sediment and rock had collected above and pressed down. Even the skulls—solid bones measuring the length and width of a grown man—were squished and twisted from the pressure.

Fortunately, the fossils were thoroughly permineralized. **Silicon** minerals in groundwater that had once flowed through the fossil layer had formed crystals within the bones' tiny holes and cracks. Now, millions of years later, even though they were cracked and broken, the bones were solid, heavy stone.

The rock in which the fossils were preserved was a combination of

Most of the summer was needed to isolate, excavate, and jacket complete skull fossils as other fossils kept getting in the way.

cement-hard siltstone, crumbly shale, and a soft, gritty clay that technicians could cut with knives. Every time it rained, the clay turned to mud. It rained often. Mud covered everything in the quarry—fossils, tools, technicians. It was often hard to see where one ended and the others began.

Whenever they could, the technicians wrapped the bones in protective layers of plaster and burlap before removing them from the bonebed. The crew treated the fossils with great care. Each fragment, no matter how small, could provide valuable clues to how *Pachyrhinosaurus* grew and lived.

Broken fossil bones that were more common were removed piece by piece. The field crew had tried gluing bits of broken bone together before removing them, but there was so much mud in the

cracks the glue would not stick. Instead, the technicians numbered each fragment, and placed all of a bone's pieces into its own plastic bag to be reassembled back in the lab.

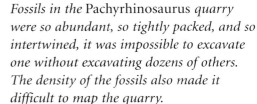

Fossils in the Pachyrhinosaurus *quarry were so abundant, so tightly packed, and so intertwined, it was impossible to excavate one without excavating dozens of others. The density of the fossils also made it difficult to map the quarry.*

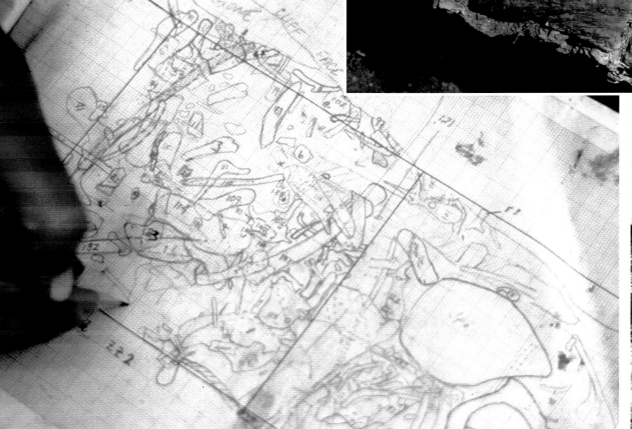

Horned Dinosaur Tales:
Attack

Sprawled among tree trunks and bushes along the riverbank, the teenaged pachyrhinosaurs slept. Some rested heads on friends' shoulders and hips; others simply touched legs and backs. The hot, mid-day sun filtered through the leaves. Steam rose from the ground. Insects settled on the dinosaurs' twitching hides to feed, then flew again, their beating wings a high-pitched lullaby in the heat. Even the birds were still.

The young *Pachyrhinosaurus* dreamed. She dreamed of mud baths and of tree trunks to scratch against. She dreamed of tasty lilies and tender, sweet, coiled shoots of young ferns. She dreamed of a family that was always there … even when the family chased you away … The young dinosaur stirred. Her eyes half-opened. She dreamed of family travelling together, feeding together, protecting one another. She

At the Scene of the Crime

Like detectives investigating a crime scene, palaeontologists gather as much evidence as possible from a fossil site. They face a daunting task. The mysteries they hope to solve happened millions of years ago. Most of the evidence that could tell them what happened has changed or been destroyed. There are no witnesses to question or help with the investigation.

Palaeontologists take great care to gather the clues that remain. To do this, they use collection techniques developed more than 100 years ago to protect fossil specimens and evidence.

When field staff collect fossils, they uncover only enough of a specimen to determine its outline and

position. The fossils are measured and mapped, and samples of the encasing rock are collected. Palaeontologists analyze this information to determine the fossil's age, how the animal died, and how it was preserved.

Crews then dig a **trench** around the specimen, and **jacket** the fossil in plaster-soaked burlap. Fossils are removed from the ground in blocks, which protect and support fragile bones.

Although the techniques work well at most fossil sites, they did not work at the Pipestone Creek bonebed. With as many as 150 bones tangled together in each square metre of the quarry, field crews could not isolate fossils, and trenching around even the largest specimens involved sorting out hundreds of other bones. They adapted collection methods to deal with a problem few palaeontologists face: too many bones.

dreamed of four hungry sickle-claw dromaeosaurs sneaking through bushes and trees toward her family. She dreamed of another three appearing from behind a shrub, sniffing and watching her and her family as they snoozed peacefully … unaware …

The young dinosaur sprang up—suddenly wide awake—and bellowed. The sickle-claws were real! One sprang through the air. It landed on a brother before he could rise to his feet. Another slashed at a sister's face, slicing her cheek and eye. A third sank its teeth into another sister's shoulder and plunged its cutting claws deep into her leg.

They kept coming, six, eight, twelve sickle-claws …

Panicking, the young dinosaur ducked under one leaping predator, and felt its claws rake her hip. She dashed through the fighting, darting this way and that. Three cousins tore out of the thicket toward the main herd; she was following them when she felt blinding, burning pain pierce her back. She threw herself against a tree, and scraped the attacker off. She swung around to face it.

Snarling, it wove from side to side, trying to make her turn and show her vulnerable sides. Instead, she lowered her head and tracked the predator with her eyes. Her frill shielded her neck and shoulders from the animal. The sickle-claw shrieked and darted forward, but she tossed it aside. It hit a tree, and fell to the ground.

Turning, she saw most of her friends fighting off the predators. A few—brothers, sisters, and cousins—were less lucky. Three tried to rise. One lay still.

The *Pachyrhinosaurus*'s vision narrowed. Blood pounded in her ears. She rushed the sickle-claws, bellowing loudly for help. She scooped one meat-eater up with her beak and threw it through the air. She turned to the next one. Her nestmates and cousins joined her.

The sickle-claws fled. Three-year-old pachyrhinosaurs might lack the long, deadly horns of their parents, but they were not defenceless.

Eat ...

Some scientists believe horned dinosaurs ate plants such as palm and **cycad** leaves. The dinosaurs' batteries of scissor-like teeth were ideal for cutting the tough, stringy greenery. However, in many places where horned dinosaur fossils are most common, palm and cycad fossils are rare.

Other palaeontologists think *Pachyrhinosaurus* and other horned dinosaurs used their teeth to snip and chop the rapidly diversifying crop of flowering plants growing across North America. They believe the success and variety of horned dinosaurs across North America during the Late Cretaceous is tied to the spread of flowering plants across the continent at the same time. Horned dinosaurs and their duckbill-dinosaur relatives may have simply taken advantage of a new, abundant food source that older kinds of dinosaurs did not know what to do with.

... And Be Eaten

When trying to figure out how dinosaurs behaved and what they ate, scientists rely on evidence preserved in the fossil record. They look for and examine bitemarks on bone, partly healed injuries, meat-eating-dinosaur teeth in plant-eating-dinosaur bonebeds, and trackways showing meat-eating dinosaurs following other dinosaurs.

To better understand how ancient animals interacted, scientists also study animals alive today. For example, Cape

The first flowering plants appeared about 100 million years ago. By the end of the Age of Dinosaurs, 65 million years ago, descendants of those pioneers—lilies, gingers, maples, and other broadleaved plants—had spread around the world. Some scientists think horned and duckbilled dinosaurs, which appeared at about the same time as the first flowering plants, may have helped the new kind of plant spread by trampling slower-growing, more ancient plants such as palms, cycads, and conifers.

If the way modern animals behave is any clue to dinosaur behaviour, healthy tyrannosaurs probably avoided healthy, adult horned dinosaurs. Young, old, sick, or injured animals were easier, safer meals.

buffalo could be considered modern equivalents for horned dinosaurs. Both are large, abundant, herding eaters of low-growing plants. Lions, the biggest, most powerful predators in Africa today, are living models for large, meat-eating dinosaurs such as *Tyrannosaurus rex* or *Albertosaurus*. Lions almost never attack herding Cape buffalo. Nine out of every 10 Cape buffalo killed by lions are old, solitary males forced out of the herd by younger, stronger rivals. Even when a lion pride selects its victim carefully, the buffalo may survive the encounter. The lions may not.

If dinosaur predators behaved as their modern counterparts do, meat-eating hunters such as *Tyrannosaurus rex* or *Albertosaurus* likely restricted their horned dinosaur snacks to young, old, sick, or weak individuals—animals that weren't as much work to kill as healthy, strong, dangerous adults.

Young horned dinosaurs were probably very vulnerable. Fossil *Protoceratops* [proh-toh-SAIR-uh-tops] nests in Asia contain as many as 40 eggs each. Wild herbivores today reproduce many more young than actually survive to adulthood. Most offspring give in to disease, starvation, accidents, injury, and predators while still young. If an animal is lucky, it will produce one or two offspring to carry on the family line. Additional offspring are gravy ... or steak for predators.

Wrap-up at Pipestone Creek

McCabe finished trenching around his *Pachyrhinosaurus* skull in late August— 11 weeks after he had discovered its frill. But before he could ship the fossil to the museum in Drumheller, he had to jacket the top and sides in burlap and plaster, cut out the rock under the block, and flip it over. Then he had to jacket the newly exposed side of the skull block. He had weeks of work left.

Tanke had not yet completely cleared the trench around his skull fossil. Once he did that, he too had to plaster, undercut, and flip the fossil block.

The season was drawing to an end, and the technicians were told to hurry. Palaeontologist Philip Currie advised McCabe and Tanke to sacrifice less important bones to collect the skulls before the weather turned bad.

McCabe and Tanke plastered hundreds of burlap bandages onto the massive fossils. Each skull-and-field-jacket block weighed more than 200 kilograms—as much as three grown men. They were so heavy the technicians could barely flip them. McCabe and Tanke dragged the blocks to the cliff edge and slid them down a long plywood ramp to the bottom. An all-terrain vehicle carried them, one by one, along the dry creekbed to the field camp. There, the technicians loaded the fossils onto a trailer with the other 300 *Pachyrhinosaurus* bones they had collected from the quarry that summer, and hauled them to Drumheller.

Each skull was wrapped in layers of burlap and plaster to protect it during the move from quarry to museum.

McCabe and Tanke built a plywood slide down which they lowered the skulls from the quarry to the creekbed. From there, an all-terrain vehicle carried the fossils to camp, where they were loaded into a truck and hauled to Drumheller.

Royal Tyrrell Museum field crews worked on the *Pachyrhinosaurus* bonebed for four summers. When the quarry closed for the last time in August 1989, 13 skulls and almost 3,000 bones had been shipped to Drumheller.

In order to reach the quarry, technicians had to climb up the bank from the creek. When it rained, the path turned treacherous, and mud coated everything in the bonebed. Rain closed the quarry for days at a time

Preparation

Assembling Pieces

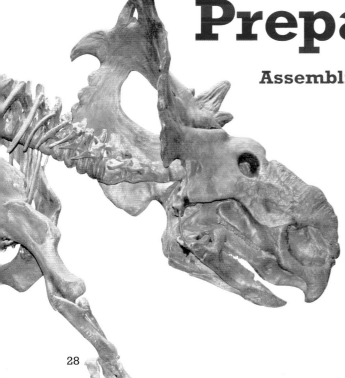

At the end of each day during the field season, technicians returned to camp with backpacks filled with fossils. Rain often kept the crew from the bonebed for days at a time. To keep busy, they **prepared** fossils.

After soaking the fossils in buckets of water to soften clay clinging to the bones, technicians brushed off the sticky, gritty mud. Sometimes a fossil required several soaks. Sometimes the person preparing the specimen needed to use dental picks or power tools to remove harder rock.

Then the technician rebuilt the fossil, carefully gluing pieces together and filling gaps with plaster. If the specimen was fragile or scientifically important, the technician applied preservative to strengthen and seal the bone.

It could take days to prepare and repair one bone. The crew prepared only a fraction of the fossils from the quarry. Most were shipped unprepared to the museum in Drumheller.

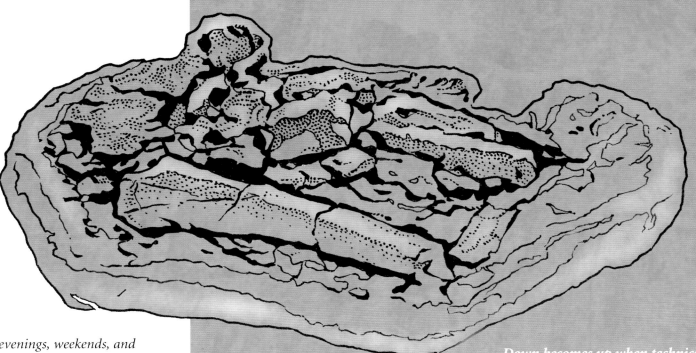

Field crews spent evenings, weekends, and rainy days preparing fossils at the camp. A preparation tent containing equipment and supplies to clean, preserve, and repair fossils sheltered both crew and fossils.

Flip Side

Down becomes up when technicians prepare dinosaur skeletons in the lab. The side of the specimen that had faced down when it was in the ground faces up in the lab, and is prepared first.

Tanke knew a great deal about the Pipestone Creek skulls before he prepared them. Field crews had uncovered enough of them to determine how much of each fossil was there and how each was positioned within the ground.

When preparing a specimen in the lab, technicians free the less-known side from rock first. They remove the plaster jacket on the side of the fossil that had faced down when it was in the field, and leave the rest of the jacket to cradle the specimen. This protects parts of the specimen that had been exposed in the field, and eases preparation of the less-known side.

When the specimen is completely prepared on one side, the preparation technician replaces the jacket and turns the specimen over. Then technicians finish preparing the fossil.

The amount of information that scientists learn from a fossil depends on how carefully it is prepared. As scientists or technicians pick away everything that is not bone, they watch for other fossils contained within the rock, surface detail on bones, and unexpected discoveries such as broken bones, skin impressions, bite marks, or irregular growths.

29

Horned Dinosaur Tales:
Food for Predators

Ranging farther from the herd in search of pastures less picked over, the teenaged pachyrhinosaurs watched from a distance as their newest siblings hatched. They watched as mothers brought tender greens for the babies to eat. They watched as babies left the nests.

Seven clutches of eggs had been laid and, despite egg-stealing predators, almost 200 babies had hatched. Many infants died within days, left defence-less when mothers went to find food. Large lizards, sickle-clawed dinosaurs, and other predators lurked nearby, ready to dash in and dine on baby pachyrhinosaur. Even two-year-olds were easy meals for predators.

But when the babies finally left the

nests, the herd could stay safely together when it searched for food.

Although banished from the breeding grounds during the nesting season, teenagers were now allowed to rejoin the family. The *Pachyrhinosaurus* and her friends took up position on the edges of the herd, forming part of a shield of bodies around the babies.

The family began to move. It had spent almost three months in the breeding grounds, anchored by nests and hatchlings. The dinosaurs had stripped the area of everything edible. Young horned dinosaurs grew quickly and ate constantly. Drawn by fresh greenery, the dinosaurs ate their way across the river basin that was their home.

Predators shadowed them. They moved when the family moved. They stopped when the family stopped. They watched and waited. They waited for youngsters to stray and for older dinosaurs to drop their guard. Toothy troodontids skulked among ferns and bushes, slipping through the ring of adults to snatch babies. Once, a flying reptile dropped out of the sky and grabbed a baby from its mother's side.

The most worrisome predator was *Daspletosaurus*, one of the massive tyrannosaurs that hunted throughout the family's summer territories. Although pachyrhinosaurs were safe when they remained together, *Daspletosaurus* could easily take on adults that were alone or in small groups.

One day, the young *Pachyrhinosaurus* saw *Daspletosaurus* burst out of a nearby thicket and charge three old

bulls trailing the herd. Around her, the family became instantly alert, lowering heads and raising frills. They edged into position, standing guard around the youngsters.

The bulls noticed the predator bearing down on them. They turned to fight. The *Daspletosaurus* singled out one of the bulls. Old and scarred, the bull had ruled over the family herd until earlier that year. He had reigned over cows and youngsters, and bullied everyone who went near him. He may have been the young *Pachyrhinosaurus's* uncle; he may have been her father—there was no way of knowing. Ever since he had lost a fight with a younger, stronger bull during the mating season, he had been exiled to the edge of the herd to live with other single, low-ranking bulls.

Snapping and lunging, the *Daspletosaurus* separated him from the others.

The old dinosaur slowly gave way. Ducking to keep clear of the predator's razor-sharp teeth, he was forced, step by reluctant step, to the side.

He darted away, trying to shake off the meat-eater. *Daspletosaurus* followed. It snapped at the bull, narrowly missing.

The old dinosaur dashed toward the herd, the predator right behind. This time, the *Daspletosaurus* did not miss. It sank its teeth into the dinosaur's hip. The bull howled and swung to face the predator. He lowered his head and raised his frill. He charged.

The *Daspletosaurus* leapt aside, and struck again. The bull stumbled, then righted himself. He spun and charged again.

Again, the predator sprang aside and its jaws snapped down.

The old bull kept moving, limping, stumbling around to face the predator. Again and again, he confronted the beast. Again and again, massive jaws tore at the old dinosaur. Finally, the *Daspletosaurus* drew away ... to wait.

Seeing his way suddenly clear, the old bull staggered towards the herd. He stopped. For several minutes, he stood weaving and shaking. His legs slowly gave way, and he sank to the ground.

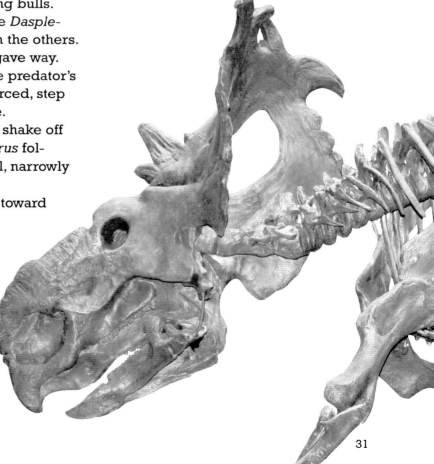

The Leg Bone Connects to the Hip Bone

One winter, while working in the lab at the Royal Tyrrell Museum, Tanke began to reconstruct a *Pachyrhinosaurus* skeleton from the Pipestone Creek fossils.

He went through the bones that had been prepared in Grande Prairie. He laid them out as a spread-eagled dinosaur skeleton. This showed him which bones were missing. He needed 21 ribs for each side of the dinosaur's chest. He needed 12 bones for the spine along the dinosaur's back, eight for the neck, and 77 smaller ones for the tail. Foot and toe bones numbered

Although many of the skulls from the bonebed were complete or nearly complete, each required extensive preparation and repairs. Pieces needed to be fitted together, and gaps where bone was missing filled in.

More than 200 single bones were cleaned and repaired for technicians to assemble one Pachyrhinosaurus *skeleton.*

almost 100. And then there were the leg bones, shoulder blades, ankle bones, and other bits and pieces to complete the skeleton.

Tanke searched through the collection bags of unprepared Pipestone Creek bone fragments, selecting fossils he needed. Then, every day, he prepared *Pachyrhinosaurus* bones. He worked on foot bones for weeks. Then he prepared vertebrae. Then he cleaned and repaired ribs ...

And so it went, for three winters.

By 1992, Tanke had most of the skeleton laid out. He needed a skull.

Unlike most of the fossils from the Pipestone Creek quarry, *Pachyrhinosaurus* skull bones were coated in hard siltstone that was difficult to remove. Tanke used an air scribe to prepare the skulls—a power tool that can remove the hardest rock from fossils.

Evidence for Habits and Habitat

Pipestone Creek's pachyrhinosaurs were social animals. Remains of at least 40 dinosaurs are preserved together in the bonebed. This suggests they lived together—for at least part of their lives or part of each year.

Pachyrhinosaurus joins a long line of herding horned dinosaurs. *Centrosaurus*, *Styracosaurus* [sty-RACK-oh-SOR-us], *Chasmosaurus* [KAZ-moh-SOR-us], and *Anchiceratops* [ANG-kee-SAIR-uh-TOPS] lived in groups. Bonebeds of these animals are found in Alberta, Montana, and Texas.

Palaeontologists do not know how herding horned dinosaurs such as *Pachyrhinosaurus* behaved. Their theories are based almost entirely on living animals with similar physical traits and similar food and **habitat** needs. Africa's

Cape buffalo are large, herding animals that eat plants growing low to the ground. Because of similarities in body shape, diet, and habitat to ancient Pachyrhinosaurus, *scientists sometimes use Cape buffalo as models whenspeculating about how the extinct dinosaurs behaved.*

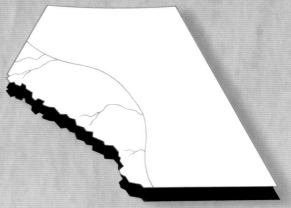

Fossil evidence shows that many horned dinosaur species may have migrated east to west and back again. However, even though there is no fossil evidence for it, it is possible some dinosaurs followed the sun north- and southward with the seasons.

Cape buffalo are modern models for herding horned dinosaurs: they, too, are large, herding plant-eaters with vast territories.

By living in groups, Cape buffalo share tasks such as protecting the herd, caring for young, and finding food. While some individuals eat or sleep, others keep eyes open for danger. If one member is threatened, the group may respond—to drive off a predator, close ranks against threats, or even nurture injured members. Among Cape buffalo, lame or sick individuals can survive for years because of group support. Young animals also benefit. In many herds, older, more experienced members of the herd position themselves around the outside of the group when feeding, resting, or travelling. Nursing mothers, youngsters, and sick and old members of the herd remain safe in the middle.

Group living affects behaviour. Members of modern herds belong to

ranks within their groups. High-ranking individuals have greater power, more food, and more opportunity to mate and have children. Males sort status by fighting, posturing, and using other ways to intimidate rivals. Large, strong, experienced males rank higher than young males. Old males that lose fights may be kicked out of the herd. Females also have a pecking order, sorted out by size, age, aggression, and number of offspring.

Living in a group allows members of a herd to specialize in certain tasks. For instance, among Cape buffalo, pathfinders guide herds between watering holes and pastures, and from summer breeding grounds to winter feeding grounds. Fighters watch for predators and rally the group to face or flee threats. Certain other members trail behind the group when it travels to keep the herd together.

Herds can also break up into smaller groups when needed. Cape buffalo gather in herds as large as 2,000 individuals on southern Africa's grasslands during the lush, rainy season. In desert-dry months, when buffalo retreat to woodlands where there is more food, the larger herd breaks into smaller groups of females and youngsters. Males form their own herds. When rains return and food becomes plentiful, the animals regroup for the birthing and breeding season.

However, information about how modern animals behave provides only clues to how extinct animals behaved. Scientists use the information to form theories about dinosaur behaviour.

Living in a group is easier and safer than living solo. Friends and family can watch for enemies while you eat or sleep. They can protect you when you are in danger, and they can force threats to disappear.

To prove their theories, they must look to evidence preserved within the fossil record.

Occasional evidence exists. For instance, a survey of more than 20 bonebeds and other fossil sites across southern Alberta shows some horned dinosaurs may have **migrated** from east to west and back again every year. Each kind of horned dinosaur seems to have travelled in a territorial band about 300 kilometres wide—no *Centrosaurus* fossils, for instance, have yet been found north or south of the *Centrosaurus*-migration band. Royal Tyrrell Museum scientist David Eberth believes the dinosaurs spent the stormy wet season in the western highlands where food was plentiful at that

time of year and storms less destructive. He thinks the dinosaurs returned to the coastal plain at the start of the hot, dry season when bad weather had passed, and food was perhaps becoming scarce in the hill country.

The fossil evidence points to east-west migration, but does not rule out north-south travel. Philip Currie thinks some species may have migrated by following the coastal plain northward and back every year. *Pachyrhinosaurus* fossils, known from southern Alberta as well as from Pipestone Creek, have also been found in Alaska. This has led some scientists to believe thick-nosed horned dinosaurs migrated to the Arctic from southern Alberta with the seasons, perhaps to take advantage of intense summer plant growth in the far north. However, the Alaska, southern Alberta, and Pipestone Creek pachyrhinosaurs are different species, and the span of time between the Pipestone Creek fossils and the other pachyrhinosaurs far exceeds the usual species lifetime. The range of *Pachyrhinosaurus* fossils across land and time does not prove north-south migration; however, it shows the dinosaurs were adaptable.

Northern horned dinosaurs may have travelled to the Arctic and back again every year. Cool northern temperatures and low winter-light levels would have forced many plants to lose their leaves, creating food shortages for the herbivorous dinosaurs. Hunger may have prompted migration. Until scientists discover more evidence, we will not know for sure.

Discoveries

Frills and Thrills of a New Thick-Nose

Frill decoration is unique to each species of horned dinosaur, but until Tanke and McCabe found complete skulls with frills attached at the Pipestone Creek bonebed, nobody knew what a *Pachyrhinosaurus* frill looked like. The fossils showed large spikes sweeping from the top to the sides, smaller horns curving toward each other between, and a line of bumps and spikes growing down the forehead.

A nose horn made of keratin would have weighed little compared to a horn made of bone. It could have grown in any shape, or to any size. If damaged, it would eventually replace itself.

The Pipestone Creek bonebed proved this Pachyrhinosaurus *had a headdress as elaborate as that found on any horned dinosaur. Sweeping spikes and curling horns once crowned the animals.*

However, Pipestone Creek fossils answer questions about frills only for Pipestone Creek pachyrhinosaurs. By analyzing skull material and other fossils from the site, palaeontologists determined the fossils were those belonging to a new species of *Pachyrhinosaurus*. Unlike specimens found elsewhere, the Pipestone Creek dinosaur has fewer **fused** vertebrae in its neck and is smaller than southern relatives.

Horns of Horn

Fossil evidence suggests the bony nose and eyebrow platforms of adult *Pachyrhinosaurus* supported horns made of … horn. Keratin, or horn, is a tough, lightweight protein. Human fingernails are made of it. Bird beaks are made of it. Rhinoceros horns are also made of it.

A body uses nutrients from blood to grow and maintain keratin. Tiny, distinctive grooves and openings riddle the surface of bones that support keratin. Blood vessels follow the channels to bring nutrients to keratin and keep it

Some pachyrhinosaurs had bowl-shaped nose platforms. Others had round nose platforms. Scientists speculate platform shape may indicate whether the dinosaur was male or female.

healthy. The bones that support a bird's beak contain these tiny channels. The bony nose platform that grows a rhinoceros's horn contains these channels. The fossilized nose and eyebrow pads of Pipestone Creek *Pachyrhinosaurus* also contain what seem to be blood-vessel channels.

Based on evidence from some fossil specimens, some palaeontologists now believe that *Pachyrhinosaurus*'s entire face was sheathed in keratin, just as fingernails cover the end of a finger.

Variations on a Theme

Although more than 50 horned dinosaur bonebeds exist in Alberta, only the Pipestone Creek site contains complete skulls. Dozens of separated skull bones and 13 complete or nearly complete skulls with joined bones show some pachyrhinosaurs at Pipestone Creek had as many as three bony spikes down the middle of their foreheads, while

others had only one. Spikes on frills also vary in length and point in different directions. Differences in the shapes of the nose and eyebrow platforms suggest adult male pachyrhinosaurs may have looked different from adult females.

Variety among the Pipestone Creek skull material indicates how individual dinosaurs may differ from one another, and still belong to the same species.

The Look of Youth

Tanke discovered a frill bone at Pipestone Creek that he thought must belong to ***Monoclonius*** [monn-oh-CLOH-nee-us], a small horned dinosaur found only in southern Alberta and Montana. He was astounded that *Monoclonius* had travelled so far from its usual territory. However, when the crew found more of the delicate, pie-crust-edged frill bones at Pipestone Creek, it became clear the *Monoclonius* bone was actually part of a juvenile *Pachyrhinosaurus* skull. Based on material in the bonebed, palaeontologists now believe youngsters of different horned dinosaur species looked alike. It wasn't until they grew up that features unique to each species appeared.

Another surprise from the Pipestone Creek bonebed was that young pachyrhinosaurs had small blades of horn on their noses and little bony bumps over their eyes. The delicate nose horns split and were partially reabsorbed into the skulls when the dinosaurs became adults, growing into the gnarly bone eyebrow and nose pads of adult pachyrhinosaurs.

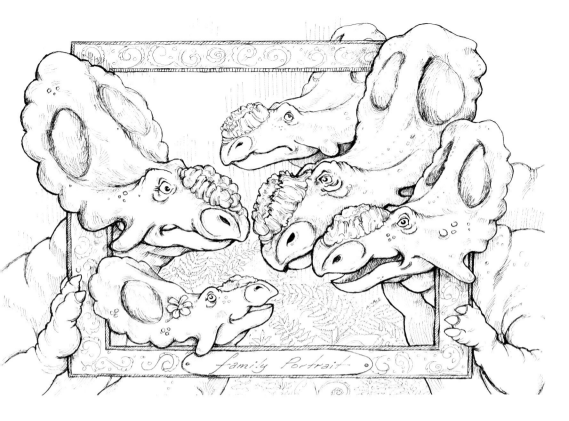

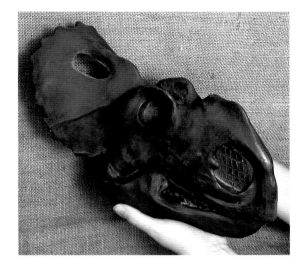

The bonebed shows that, unlike adult pachyrhinosaurs, young Pachyrhinosaurus *had a bony horn on its nose.*

Pachyrhinosaurus *seems to have grown up in four years. The bonebed contains remains of pachyrhinosaurs as small as German shepherd dogs and as large as Jeeps.*

The Pachyrhinosaurus *bonebed shows how dinosaurs that are brothers, sisters, aunts, and uncles can still look very different from each other.*

How Does Your Dinosaur Grow?

At least four sizes of pachyrhinosaurs are preserved in the Pipestone Creek bonebed. Scientists believe bones in the smallest size-group come from pachyrhinosaurs born the same year they died. The animals would have been about the size of German shepherd dogs. The next size-group represents what may be dinosaurs that died in their second year. The third group may stand for third-year pachyrhinosaurs. It includes remains of what seem to be the herd's teenagers.

The bones share many features with fossils from the bonebed's smaller—younger—size-groups. They also show traits of adult pachyrhinosaurs, including small forehead and frill spikes, and the transformation of small nose and eyebrow horns found on young *Pachyrhinosaurus* skulls into bony adult facial platforms.

Adult pachyrhinosaurs make up the fourth and largest size-group. Their skull bones are cemented together, unlike those of the smaller groups. The fossils have spikes, forehead horns and well-developed frills, and broad, gnarly pads of bone on their noses and eyebrows.

Frills and Furbelows

Horns, spikes, face bumps, and frill scallops may have evolved in horned dinosaurs as a way for adults to attract mates and scare off rivals. These features appeared only as horned dinosaurs approached adult size, suggesting ties to adult behaviour.

Palaeontologists once thought the horns and ornamentation evolved solely as defence against predators. However, young horned dinosaurs lacked not only well-developed frills and long horns, but also the bulk and experience of their parents. Young horned dinosaurs would have greatly needed fighting horns, intimidating war bonnets, and bony neck shields, but these features must have also served purposes specific to mature animals.

Adult horned dinosaurs may have used these features to change tyrannosaur dinner plans, but scaring off predators would have been a handy secondary use. Impressing females, maintaining rank within a herd and carrying around personal nametags on their heads so other members of the herd could recognize them at a distance would have been important everyday uses for horns and ornaments. If frills were brightly coloured, they would have made especially effective gender and status advertisements. However, colour rarely

Horned dinosaurs may have used their horns to wrestle or charge rivals. Few horned dinosaur fossils of any species preserve bone injuries that indicate outright spearing and fighting with horns.

Spikes, horns, and even colour on a horned dinosaur headdress may have helped individuals recognize each other from a distance.

fossilizes, so we will never know how showy horned dinosaurs really were.

Male and female horned dinosaurs had similar bony horns and ornaments, as is often found among many large, herding animals alive today. Pipestone Creek skulls, however, sport one of two kinds of nose and eyebrow platforms: bowl-shaped or rounded. Platform shape may indicate whether an animal was male or female. The number of spikes on a *Pachyrhinosaurus's* forehead may also provide clues to gender. Many adult skulls with one spike were discovered, compared to only a few with three. In modern herds, females always outnumber adult males. Single forehead spikes on Pipestone Creek skulls may indicate female pachyrhinosaurs, while three-spike foreheads may represent adult males.

Each species of horned dinosaur sported its own unique combination of horns and frill decoration.

D.Moh
04

Horned Dinosaur Tales:
On the Move

Cooler nights, increasing rains, and shorter days signalled time to return to the hill country. Storms brewed on the plain, growing suddenly from daily showers into day-long downpours. The family turned toward safer, drier winter territories.

The group moved quickly. The bulls felt no need to fight among themselves for rank or mates at this time of year. The cows were undistracted by nesting or mating needs. The herd stopped to eat and drink only at dusk. Each dinosaur lost weight as it toiled westward. Unable to sustain the pace and scant food rations, many of the youngest herd members fell behind and disappeared. Despite that, the herd grew steadily as more families joined them.

They hurried. The hill country did not flood as the plain did. When rain fell in the hills, it brought life to what was dry and barren during the summer. Water drained quickly away, filling waterways that now blocked the dinosaurs' route across the plain. There, storms turned streams into torrents. Currents cut away at creek banks and swept trees downstream. Ponds flooded and spread over the soggy landscape.

The dinosaurs reached the river late one morning. Swift and swollen, the water rushed toward the sea. The young *Pachyrhinosaurus* could barely see the other side, hundreds of metres away.

The herd's leaders turned upstream, drawing the other dinosaurs along. The pathfinders had travelled the route between summer breeding grounds and winter feeding grounds many, many times during the years. For days, they led the herd beside the river, pausing frequently, allowing stragglers to catch up, gathering more families. Around the *Pachyrhinosaurus,* thousands of horned dinosaurs mustered and moved upstream.

The herd came to one of the river's tributaries, flowing from the west to dump its water into the wider watercourse. The dinosaurs followed it. The river narrowed.

One morning, the pathfinders plunged into the water and swam for the other bank. Within minutes, dinosaurs choked the river. The young *Pachyrhinosaurus* scrambled down to the water's edge. Other dinosaurs crowding behind pushed her into the water. The current tugged at her. She spun around, bumping into dinosaurs all around her. Pointing her beak upstream and across the river, she started to swim.

Ahead, a group of babies panicked as the current grabbed them. Gasping and bawling, they thrashed and tried to climb onto other dinosaurs' backs. Several slipped and went under. One resurfaced beside the young *Pachyrhinosaurus,* scrabbling at her side and choking. She nudged it with her beak, trying to help. The little dinosaur went under again. She felt it tangle among her legs … then it was gone.

Wedged among other dinosaurs, she continued to swim.

Finally her toes raked muddy ground. She pulled herself out of the river and up the bank.

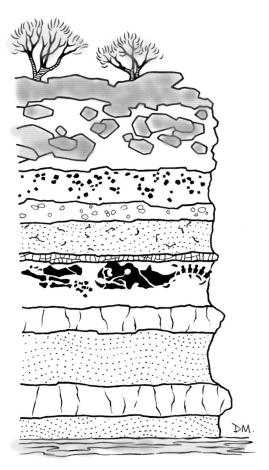

The layers of rock beneath the bonebed represent an ancient river system. Alternating sandstones, siltstones, and shales speak of a wide, slow river that wound across a low-lying plain. The river changed course often, forcing new channels and streams through a maze of sandbanks, ponds, and marshes. The dark silt-stone, shale, and clay rock of the fossil layer may be remains of mud from when the river spilled over its low banks to flood the surrounding countryside.

Death of a Herd

By studying the Pipestone Creek bonebed and other fossil sites, palaeontologists have pieced together a picture of what may have happened to *Pachyrhinosaurus* 76 million years ago.

The dinosaurs lived in herds. During four years of excavating at Pipestone Creek, the Royal Tyrrell Museum of Palaeontology collected almost 3,000 bones from the Pipestone Creek quarry—99 percent of which are *Pachyrhinosaurus* fossils. For these bones to be preserved together, the dinosaurs had to have died together. If they died together, they probably lived together.

Pipestone Creek cuts through the middle of the Pachyrhinosaurus *bonebed. More than 100 metres downstream from the quarry, the fossil layer continues into the creek's opposite bank.*

Remains of at least 40 individuals were found in the quarry. More than 100 metres downstream, the bonebed continues into the creek's opposite bank. During countless years, more than 6,000 cubic metres of the fossil layer—untold numbers of bones—were washed away as the creek cut through the bonebed. By extending the number of animals found in the quarry to the entire bonebed area, as many as a few thousand pachyrhinosaurs may have

died 76 million years ago at what is now Pipestone Creek. Because of erosion caused by the creek, we will never know how many animals were once preserved there, nor how much of the original herd the fossils represent.

Based on evidence, scientists think a large herd of at least several hundred pachyrhinosaurs drowned when a nearby river flooded the area. Large, fearsome tyrannosaurs and sickle-clawed dromaeosaurs fed on the rotting carcasses, leaving behind teeth and bitemarks on bone. A second flood mixed the bones and buried them in a thick layer of mud.

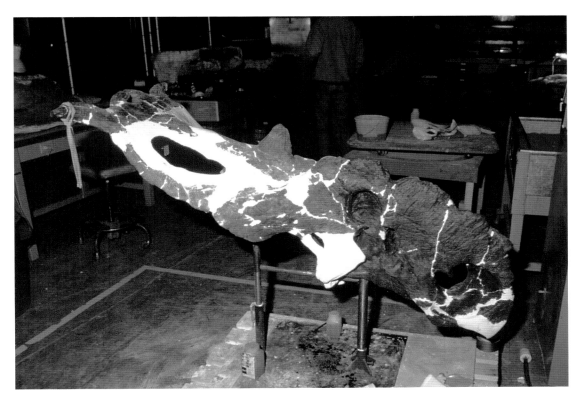

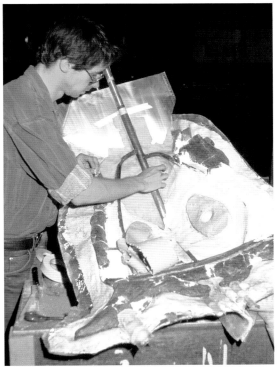

Tanke molded the Pachyrhinosaurus *skull by painting layers of latex onto each side of the fossil. A fibreglass jacket helped the flexible mold keep its shape while a cast was made.*

Display

Two Heads Are Better Than One

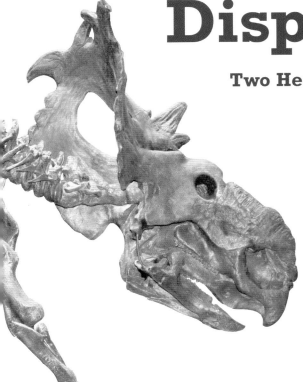

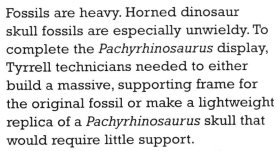

Fossils are heavy. Horned dinosaur skull fossils are especially unwieldy. To complete the *Pachyrhinosaurus* display, Tyrrell technicians needed to either build a massive, supporting frame for the original fossil or make a lightweight replica of a *Pachyrhinosaurus* skull that would require little support.

They decided to make a replica.

Using one of the Pipestone Creek skulls he had prepared earlier, Tanke brushed liquid latex onto one side. When the latex dried, he painted

another layer, then another layer, and another layer … The flexible rubber **mold** thickened. When it was more than two centimetres thick, technicians fitted a fibreglass jacket to the specimen to hold and stiffen the mold.

Once an exact copy of the fossil was made from the mold, technicians needed to paint it to look like the original fossil.

They flipped the skull block over, and painted latex on the other side of the fossil.

It took months for Tanke and the other technicians to finish. They removed the fibreglass jackets. Removing the two halves of the latex mold was a greater challenge. The technicians gently pulled them off the skull, lifting them centimetre by careful centimetre. They wanted the mold to maintain as many details and textures of the *Pachyrhinosaurus* skull as possible. A latex mold can retain almost all of the surface detail found on a fossil if it is carefully made and removed.

The latex peeled off the specimen as if it were dinosaur skin.

Inspection of the mold showed no damage. Technicians replaced the mold halves into the supporting jackets. Then they **cast** the specimen. Because they wanted the replica skull to weigh as little as possible, they used a liquid plastic resin that hardens when exposed to air. For three days, they painted layer after layer of resin onto the insides of the mold, waiting for each layer to dry before adding another.

When technicians removed the jackets and molds a second time, they uncovered two perfect half-casts of the *Pachyrhinosaurus* skull.

They glued the halves together, and sanded down the seams where they joined. Brown, grey, red, and yellow paint dabbed and brushed over a base coat of purple paint provides depth of colour to the cast. The replica skull looks exactly like a complete, original *Pachyrhinosaurus* skull, but has only a fraction of the fossil's mass.

Bone Clones

A fossil is a one-of-a-kind relic from the past. While a horned dinosaur rib or tyrannosaur tooth may look much like hundreds of other such fossils, each is unique. Each has the potential to offer new insight into extinct creatures and answer scientists' questions about ancient worlds. Complete fossil skulls, skeletons, or rare animals are especially valuable for the information they provide.

However, fossils are fragile. Constant handling and even the slight temperature or humidity changes within a room cause fossils to slowly break apart. Palaeontologists make replicas, or casts, of fossils out of durable materials such as resin, plastic foam, fiberglass, and even plaster to keep valuable specimens safe. A cast can contain all the surface detail found on an original fossil and can be handled much more easily and safely. By making many cast-copies of a single fossil, more scientists can do more research on one fossil at one time.

Casts also help museums exhibit ancient animals in realistic poses. Fossil bones are heavy. They need to be supported by sturdy clips and braces. If you try drilling into fossils or screwing bolts into them, they may shatter. This limits how dinosaur skeletons can be displayed. Few three-dimensional skeletons made from real fossils are shown as if the skeletons were running, jumping, or fighting. Most have four feet planted on the ground, and are well braced by steel rods and posts.

By using casts, exhibit makers can arrange a skeleton in any position. They can thread steel braces through replica fossils. They can drill holes into cast bones. They can bolt them into place. Fewer braces and supports are needed to support casts than fossils.

Many dinosaur skeletons displayed in museums are replicas. The Pipestone Creek *Pachyrhinosaurus* is one of the exceptions at the Royal Tyrrell Museum.

The number of fossils from Pipestone Creek and the thoroughness of the bones' permineralization gave the museum an option it does not have with isolated, one-of-a-kind fossils. The museum built a display using original Pipestone Creek fossils for everything but the skull and hip area.

Fossil casts allow museums to display dinosaur skeletons in more realistic poses than are possible using original fossils. Once painted, the replica bones look like the real thing.

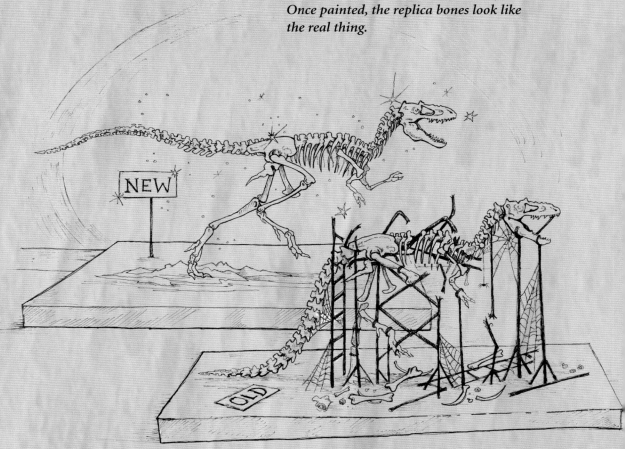

45

Horned Dinosaur Tales:
Storm

The first big storm of the season swept down upon the dinosaurs. Wind tore branches from trees and flattened fields. Blasting in from the sea, it drove sheets of rain sideways across the river plain. It pushed the dinosaurs westward on their path.

It blew so hard, it stoppered the rivers. Rain and river water piled up against the storm surge. It spilled over riverbanks. It burst through sand levees. It flowed across the plain. Ponds and marshes swelled into lakes, and still the storm blew.

The flood forced the dinosaurs to change their path. They broke into smaller groups and began to weave across the plain, searching out higher ground as they headed west.

Families became separated. Mothers lost their children. Children lost their siblings.

The wind blew. The rain fell. More and more of the plain flooded.

The dinosaurs waded and swam from one refuge of high ground to another across the flooded river basin. Gentle mounds and ridges that had risen no more than a few metres above the plain a week earlier now became islands.

Hurrying along, the *Pachyrhinosaurus* was wet and chilled. She had eaten no more than a few mouthfuls of drowned weeds snatched on the run since the storm began. She had not slept—wind and driving rain made that impossible.

The rain fell. The water rose.

All around, the young *Pachyrhinosaurus* could see islands dotting the flood. Each island was packed with wet, weary dinosaurs. Each island was ringed by more dinosaurs standing ankle deep, knee deep in water, pushing, shoving, wrestling to gain the high ground.

She joined the press to climb up a muddy mound out of the water. She dug her toes into the mud and weeds to help her push her way through the other dinosaurs. She butted them with her beak, but there was no way through.

The water rose.

It climbed up her legs and belly. She had to hold her beak high to breathe. Big, strong members of the herd shouldered past onto the island, shoving the young *Pachyrhinosaurus* into deeper water.

She swam to keep afloat. If she stretched her hind legs, she could just feel the ground beneath her toes.

Still the water rose.

Panicking, a young bull threw his legs onto her back and tried to climb up to escape the water. She bellowed as she went under. She thrashed and kicked. He let go, but when she regained the surface, he pushed her under again. Another dinosaur joined him, and another ... The young *Pachyrhinosaurus* was fighting with a dozen members of her herd to keep her beak above the water, each trying to climb atop the others, each bawling in terror.

Down she went. Up she kicked. Down someone else went. Down she went again. The water boiled with panicking, thrashing, bellowing dinosaurs.

She could not breathe. She choked on water and mud. She coughed, and gasped in more water. Someone kicked her belly. Winded, she sank to the bottom, pushed and held down by bodies scrambling, flailing, piling atop her.

The *Pachyrhinosaurus* struggled, trying to dislodge the weight. She breathed more water. A dark wave swept over her eyes, dimming the light that filtered from the surface through the churning legs and mud. Her legs grew weak. Soft, black fog enveloped her and cushioned her head.

She stopped fighting. She stopped breathing.

The wind blew. The rain fell. The water rose.

The young dinosaur died.

Seasons of Storms

All was not well in Alberta's dinosaur paradise during the Late Cretaceous Period. Chains of volcanoes in British Columbia belched smoke, dust, and ash into the air. Prevailing winds from the Pacific Ocean pushed the pollution eastward, where it blanketed Alberta's coastal plain. The ash is preserved today as thick layers of clay called bentonite.

An ever-changing sea level pushed and pulled the coast of North America's inland sea across Alberta. The province was so flat that in one watery advance 74 million years ago, the sea flooded most of the province in less than 1,000 years. High sea level meant warmer temperatures on the coastal plain. It also may have combined with dust and ash from volcanoes to fuel changes in weather. Air cooled during short winter days over the western highlands flowed down across the plain to meet warm, humid air over the sea. As happens today over large bodies of warm water, the air masses would wind around each other—hot air rising, cool air sinking. The corkscrew would gather energy as more warm air rose from the sea's surface. If the sun-heated sea supplied enough energy, the system would switch into a hurricane, and spin furiously northeastwards toward the coast. Winds pounding the shoreline would dam streams already overflowing with rainfall. In a matter of days, the coastal plain hundreds of kilometres inland would be awash with storm water.

Animals stranded on the plain would

As remains of ancient volcanic eruptions, bentonite clay now helps scientists pinpoint how old rocks are. By measuring radioactive elements in clay found in a rock layer that formed after the Pipestone Creek bonebed, Tyrrell scientist Dave Eberth determined the bonebed is at least 73.5 million years old, and probably a few million years older.

have had few places to take refuge. High ground, which likely did not measure more than a few metres above sea level, would rapidly become shrinking islands in the flood. Sometimes they would disappear completely, leaving animals to drown while trying to keep their heads above water.

A cluster of 14 bonebeds across a four-kilometre stretch of the South Saskatchewan River in southern Alberta records one such storm. Together the bonebeds may preserve remains of thousands of centrosaurs that died

78 million years ago. As floodwaters receded, floating carcasses settled in low spots, forming the scattered bonebeds. The death toll was probably much higher than the number of bones found, as the modern river cuts through only a small portion of the region's Late Cretaceous rock.

An increase in extreme, unpredictable weather may have caused many floods, and many bonebeds to form, across Alberta and Montana during the last few million years of the Cretaceous Period.

Completing the Puzzle

Technicians assembled the prepared *Pachyrhinosaurus* fossils into the skeleton that would be displayed in the museum's gallery. A five-metre-long steel rod recreates the sweep of *Pachyrhinosaurus*'s back and tail. Most of the skeleton is suspended from this frame. Technicians cut, bent, and welded steel plates and bars into giant clips, and attached them to the central rod. Each clip is shaped to hold one of the specimen's backbones.

Steel plates were welded to the frame—one near the head and the other about one-third of the way from the end of the tail. Rods attached to the plates support the dinosaur's leg bones

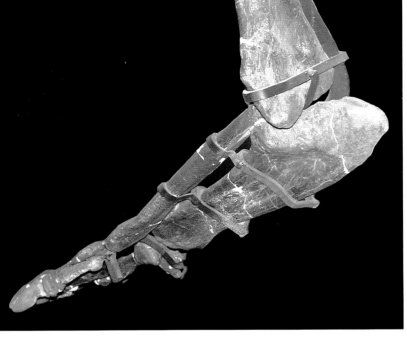

When they assembled the Pachyrhinosaurus *skeleton, technicians hung the fossils on a steel frame of braces and supports. Each clip holding a fossil was specially welded and fitted around that bone.*

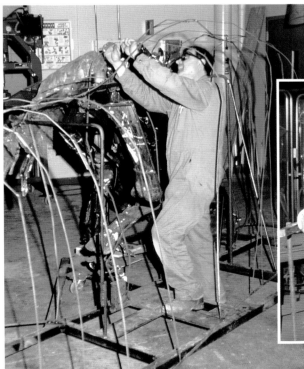

Because the ribs were twisted and bent in every direction when they fossilized, technicians had to break and reshape each rib so that it could hang smoothly from the skeleton's backbone.

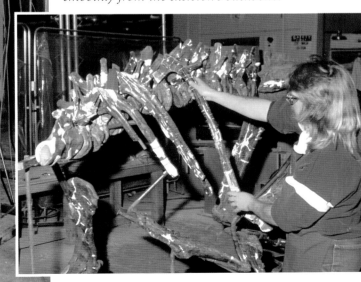

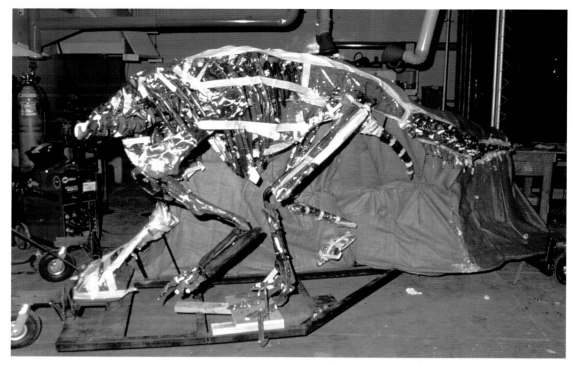

and the curving spinal frame. To avoid damaging original fossils, technicians cast part of the dinosaur's hip region. They fitted the replica around the rear plate so that part of the display could support the skeleton's tail and hind legs.

Ribs presented the biggest challenge in building the skeleton. They varied in size and shape. Each was bent and twisted in a different direction. The only way technicians could get the bones to hang in a rib cage was to break the fossils and correct their curves.

The technicians threaded braces and clips between ribs to hold the dinosaur's shoulder blades—long, flat, spatula-shaped bones. Rods and clips support *Pachyrhinosaurus*'s lifted left front leg.

A wooden frame draped in burlap and foam, and covered with sand, forms a backdrop for the skeleton.

Technicians wrapped burlap behind the skeleton and around a wooden frame, and sprayed it with foam. They then glued a thick layer of sand onto the foam.

Horned Dinosaur Tales:
Aftermath

The wind died. The rain stopped. Patches of sky cleared. The sun shone again.

A vast lake covered the river plain. Stands of trees rooted beneath the water lifted broken arms to the sky. Remains of the horned dinosaur herd crowded low-lying islands. Of the more than 6,000 dinosaurs that had crossed the river just days earlier, fewer than 2,500 lived, shivering, miserable, and hungry.

Bodies of dead pachyrhinosaurs clogged the water. They ringed the islands and floated among half-submerged trees.

The channels and streams that emptied the plain unplugged. Rivers flowed eastward once more, and the plain slowly drained. The young *Pachyrhinosaurus*'s body swirled in the receding currents, packing closer and closer with other corpses as the water sank. They filled hollows. They collected in dips. They settled into the mud.

As temperatures warmed, the smell of rotting meat rose from the muddy ground. Insects were the first to feed at the horned dinosaur buffet. A haze of insects swarmed the bodies. They chewed. They burrowed. They laid eggs. The river plain buzzed.

The sky, once black with storm clouds, now grew dark as birds and flying reptiles came to feed. The stench also drew meat-eating dinosaurs that had survived the storm. With so much meat to choose from, *Albertosaurus, Daspletosaurus, Troodon,* and **Saurornitholestes** [SOR-or-nith-oh-LESS-teez] ignored each other. Standing almost side by side, the predators slurped down innards, pulled apart skeletons, and crunched bones.

The stranded *Pachyrhinosaurus* survivors picked their way through the dead zone. They waded through puddles and trod through muck, stepping on the half-buried bodies of former herd mates. Hunting instincts dying hard, the meat-eaters growled and snarled at the passing horned dinosaurs, but no predator left feeding to chase them.

Then the last of the horned dinosaur survivors were gone, having escaped to safety in the hill country.

A few weeks later, another hurricane hit. Again the wind blew. Again the rain fell. Again the rivers stopped flowing forward and starting spreading sideways. Water and more mud flooded the bonefield and stranded the meat-eaters on high ground. The skeletons of the dead dinosaurs fell apart. Swirling currents jumbled the bones. They moved smaller bones short distances and mixed everything together.

Again the storm passed. Again the rivers and streams started flowing.

The receding water revealed a flat, muddy plain broken by battered trees and the few ridges and mounds of high ground.

The bones of the young *Pachyrhinosaurus* lay buried deep within the mud.

In the Gallery

In early spring, 1994, technicians took *Pachyrhinosaurus* for a walk. They wheeled the skeleton out of the lab, through the museum's back door and up the road to the other side of the building. Re-entering the museum through an emergency exit near the front entrance, *Pachyrhinosaurus* paraded into the gallery.

The technicians moved it into position, and bolted the display down. They refitted the *Pachyrhinosaurus* skull cast to the end of the skeleton.

A plywood platform was built around the display. Technicians sprayed it with foam, and glued down more sand to match the backdrop.

After eight years of work, Tyrrell staff completed the Pipestone Creek puzzle. They had pieced together a skeleton

The Pachyrhinosaurus *was moved into its permanent exhibit space after a brief journey outside from the museum's lab to the gallery.*

out of more than 3,000 jumbled, broken bones, and created an exhibit that helps bring the mysterious dinosaur to life.

Today, the *Pachyrhinosaurus* skeleton seems to step out of its sandstone backdrop into the gallery ...

When the skull cast was fitted to the display, the skeleton was complete. All that remained was completing the exhibit backdrop.

Glossary

Albertosaurus [al-BERT-oh-SOR-us]: Large, meat-eating dinosaur that lived from 78 million to 68 million years ago. Albertosaurus was an early, smaller cousin to Tyrannosaurus rex.

Anchiceratops [ANG-kee-SAIR-uh-tops]: Horned dinosaur with long eyebrow horns and a frill with scalloped edges.

Biology: Study of life, and of how life works.

Bonebed: Jumbled remains of many animals that collected naturally in one place.

Braincase: The part of a skull that contains the brain.

Cast: To make a three-dimensional copy from a mold; a copy made from a mold.

Catalogue: To list according to subject or description.

Centrosaurus [SEN-troh-SOR-us]: Horned dinosaur characterized by a long horn on its nose, and short horns over its eyes.

Champsosaur [CHAMP-soh-sor]: Crocodile-like reptile that existed until about 50 million years ago.

Chasmosaurus [KAZ-moh-SOR-us]: Horned dinosaur with a short horn on its nose, and large holes in the bone of its frill.

Cretaceous [kre-TAY-shus]: Geologic period dating from 140 million to 65 million years ago. The Cretaceous Period was the last period of the Age of Dinosaurs.

Cycad [SY-kad]: Ancient tropical plant that resembles a short, fat palm tree.

Daspletosaurus [dah-SPLEE-toh-SOR-us]: Large, meat-eating dinosaur that lived from 76 million to 72 million years ago. May have been the direct ancestor to Tyrannosaurus rex.

Dromaeosaur [DROH-mee-oh-sor]: Small, meat-eating dinosaur characterized by a large, crescent-shaped claw on the second toe of each hind foot.

Erode: To gradually wear away.

Fossil: Remains or trace of ancient life at least 10,000 years old.

Frill: Horned dinosaur's bony headdress that starts at the forehead and sweeps back over the neck.

Fuse: To become one.

Habitat: Place where a plant or animal lives in the wild.

Horned dinosaurs: Group of dinosaurs with bony, parrot-like beaks. Many horned dinosaurs also have triangular heads, horns on their faces, and frills on the backs of their heads.

Jacket: To wrap a fossil in protective layers of burlap and plaster.

Keratin: Tough, flexible protein that forms horn, beaks, fingernails, scales, and hair.

Migrate: To travel from one territory to another at regular times throughout the year.

Mold: Hollow, three-dimensional pattern used to create shapes.

Monoclonius [monn-oh-CLOH-nee-us]: Horned dinosaur that lived in Alberta and Montana 76 million to 73 million years ago.

Organic: Having to do with living things; made up of carbon molecules such as those found in living things.

Overburden: Rock above a specimen that must be removed in order to expose and collect a fossil.

Pachyrhinosaurus [PACK-ee-RY-noh-SOR-us]: Horned dinosaur characterized by thick, gnarled platforms of bone on the nose and eyebrows where other horned dinosaur fossils have horns. The platforms may have supported horns made of keratin.

Palaeontology: Study of ancient life through fossils. A palaeontologist is a scientist who studies ancient life through fossils.

Permineralization: Fossilization process by which groundwater minerals fill porous spaces within bone and wood.

Predator: Animal that hunts other animals for food.

Prepare: To remove rock from a fossil, repair the fossil, and seal its surface with preservative.

Protoceratops [proh-toh-SAIR-uh-tops]: Small, hornless dinosaur (but still considered a horned dinosaur) with only a small skull shelf for a frill. Most abundant in Asia, but also found in North America.

Quarry: Place where rocks containing fossils are excavated.

Replacement: Fossilization process by which organic minerals within bone or wood are replaced by inorganic minerals. It can also include the entire replacement of the original bone, wood, animal, or plant with inorganic minerals.

Saurornitholestes [SOR-or-nith-oh-LESS-teez]: Dromaeosaur that lived in Alberta during the Late Cretaceous.

Sediment: Dirt, sand, dust, and other particles deposited by wind or water.

Silicon: Mineral that makes up sand, quartz, and glass.

Species: Similar plants or animals that can mate and produce offspring that can also reproduce.

Specimen: Item that is representative of a larger group.

Styracosaurus [sty-RACK-oh-SOR-us]: Horned dinosaur with a long horn on its nose, and spikes radiating out from the edge of its frill.

Transition: Gradual change.

Trench: Ditch, or to dig a ditch.

Triceratops [try-SAIR-uh-tops]: Large, horned dinosaur with a short nose horn and a metre-long horn over each eye.

Troodon [TRUE-oh-don]: Small, meat-eating dinosaur—believed to have been among the smartest of dinosaurs.

Tyrannosaurus [ty-RAN-oh-SOR-us]: Large meat-eating dinosaur, characterized by two fingers on each of its hands. Albertosaurus, Daspletosaurus, and Tyrannosaurus are tyrannosaurs [ty-RAN-oh-sors].

Vertebra: One back bone. Vertebrae is the plural of vertebra. A vertebrate is an animal with a backbone.

Behind the Scenes

Palaeontologist **Don Brinkman** studies ancient land-dwelling **vertebrate** animals that are not dinosaurs. He determined climate in the ancient Arctic using 60-million-year-old turtle specimens, and helped trace how Asian turtles vanquished their North American cousins after dinosaurs became extinct. He is a key researcher in a southern Alberta fossil-site survey that sheds light on horned dinosaur migration and ancient climate.

By measuring radiometric isotopes in volcanic ash, sedimentary geologist **David Eberth** determined the *Pachyrhinosaurus* bonebed formed at least 73.5 million years ago, and probably a few million years earlier. With fellow scientist Don Brinkman, Eberth conducted the survey of southern Alberta horned dinosaur bonebeds and other fossil sites that provides insights into Late Cretaceous climate change and horned dinosaur herding and migration.

Darren Tanke began his career in palaeontology as a volunteer in 1979. His part in the expedition to the *Pachyrhinosaurus* bonebed in 1986 landed him a job as technician with the Tyrrell Museum the following year. In addition to working on *Pachyrhinosaurus*, he helped excavate the *Centrosaurus* and *Albertosaurus* bonebeds in Alberta, and a meat-eating dinosaur bonebed in Argentina.

Dinosaur palaeontologist **Philip Currie** began excavating Dinosaur Provincial Park's *Centrosaurus* bonebed in 1979. He has since extended his bonebed work to sites containing bones of meat-eating dinosaurs. His work on such sites in Alberta and Argentina leads him to believe that some meat-eating dinosaurs lived together in groups for at least parts of their lives.

"The best thing about working in palaeontology," says technician **Jim McCabe**, "is uncovering something unique every time you go to work." Since he started with the Tyrrell Museum in 1982, McCabe has taken part in fossil-collecting expeditions around the world. He led the 1986 expedition to the *Pachyrhinosaurus* bonebed, and was part of the team that excavated the *Centrosaurus* bonebed in Dinosaur Provincial Park.

Pachyrhinosaurus at Home

The *Pachyrhinosaurus* makes its home in the Dinosaur Hall at the Royal Tyrrell Museum of Palaeontology. Located in the heart of Alberta's dinosaur-rich badlands, the museum houses more than 40 complete dinosaur skeletons and one of the world's largest collections of fossils—ranging from 3.5-billion-year-old bacteria colonies to 11,000-year-old giant mammals. Eight staff palaeontologists and numerous visiting scientists and students study fossils stored at the museum to better understand ancient life in all its forms.

Created by Calgary artist Brian Cooley, this Pachyrhinosaurus *sculpture incorporates the theory that* Pachyrhinosaurus's *nose and eyebrow platforms supported keratin horns.*